Delivery apps are a type of gig economy job that involves picking up and delivering orders from restaurants and stores using your own vehicle. DoorDash is a popular delivery app that allows users to place orders for food, groceries, and other items from local businesses, which are then delivered by independent contractors (called "Dashers"). Working as a Dasher allows you to set your own schedule and work as much or as little as you want, making it a convenient way to earn money on your own terms.

However, working as a delivery driver also has its challenges. You are responsible for your own vehicle, gas, and maintenance costs, which can be a significant expense. You may also have to deal with difficult customers or challenging delivery situations. It is important to weigh the pros and cons of working as a delivery driver before deciding if it is the right fit for you. In this book, we will provide tips and strategies for making the most of your experience as a DoorDash driver.

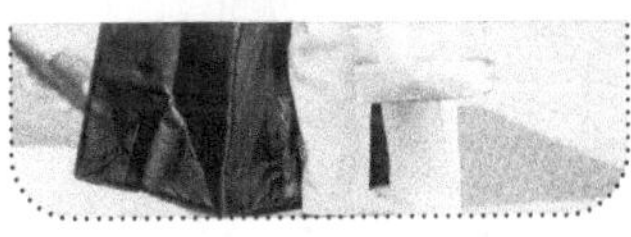

The gig economy and delivery apps are expected to continue growing in the coming years, with more and more people turning to temporary or flexible work as a source of income. The COVID-19 pandemic obviously accelerated the trend towards gig work, as many people lost traditional jobs or were seeking additional sources of income during this time.

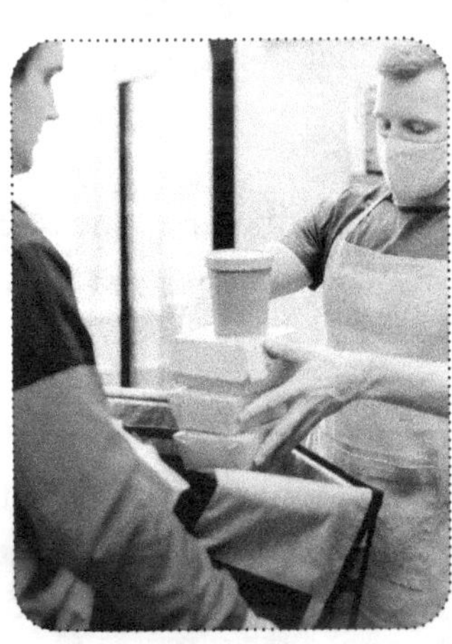

Online platforms such as DoorDash have made it easier than ever to connect with clients or customers who need specific tasks or services performed, and the convenience of being able to work on your own schedule has made gig work attractive to many people.

However, the gig economy and delivery apps have also faced criticism and controversy. Some have argued that gig work is insecure and lacks the benefits and protections of traditional employment, such as sick leave and unemployment insurance. There have also been concerns about the treatment of gig workers, with some claiming that they are not paid fairly or are not provided with adequate support and resources.

A class action lawsuit was filed against DoorDash in California in 2021 alleging that the company was paying its drivers "substandard wages." This lawsuit claimed that DoorDash violated California labor laws by failing to provide its drivers with minimum wage and overtime pay, and by misclassifying them as independent contractors rather than employees.

The plaintiffs in the lawsuit argued that DoorDash drivers should be classified as employees rather than independent contractors because they are closely controlled by the company and do not have the freedom to work for other delivery companies. They also argued that DoorDash was required to pay its drivers minimum wage and overtime pay under California law, and that the company had failed to do so.

DoorDash denied the allegations and argued that its drivers were properly classified as independent contractors.

> **"It's important to weigh the pros and cons of working as a delivery driver before deciding if this is the right fit for you."**

This class action lawsuit highlights the ongoing debate over the classification of gig economy workers and the extent to which they are entitled to the same protections and benefits as traditional employees. The outcome of this lawsuit and similar cases will have significant implications for the gig economy and the rights of gig workers across the United States.

Despite these challenges, the gig economy and delivery apps are expected to continue growing in the future. It is likely that more and more people will turn to gig work as a way to supplement their income or as a primary source of work. It is important for gig workers and the companies that rely on them to address these challenges and ensure that gig work is a fair and sustainable way of earning a living.

DoorDash Delivery: The Ultimate Getting Started Guide to Driving for Profit

By Mark H. Delfs

Table Of Contents

Chapter 1:
The Gig Economy and Delivery Apps

The gig economy refers to the trend of people working temporary or flexible jobs, often through online platforms. Delivery apps are a type of gig economy job that allows individuals to work as independent contractors, picking up and delivering orders from restaurants and stores using their own vehicle.

DoorDash is one of the leading delivery app platforms, connecting drivers with customers who need items delivered to their location. Working as a delivery driver for DoorDash can be a flexible and convenient way to earn money, but it also comes with its own set of challenges and responsibilities. In this chapter, we will explore the rise of the gig economy and the role that delivery apps play within it. We will also discuss the pros and cons of working as a delivery driver and how to decide if it is the right fit for you.

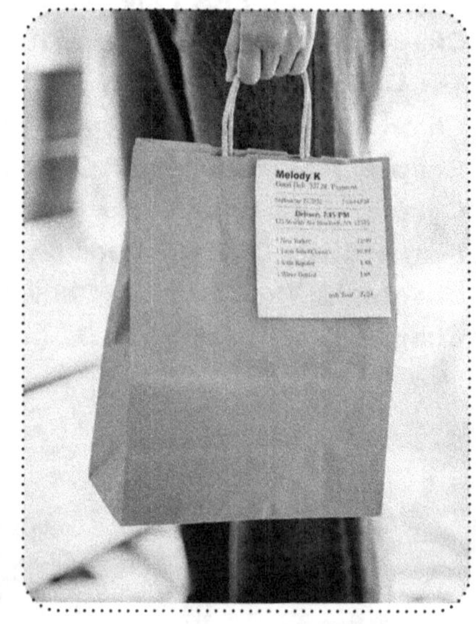

The gig economy has grown significantly in recent years, with more and more people turning to temporary or flexible work as a source of income. This trend has been fueled by the proliferation of online platforms that connect workers with clients or customers who need their services. Gig economy jobs can range from task-based jobs such as cleaning or handyman services, to more traditional freelance work such as writing or graphic design.

DoorDash as a company, has made efforts to work with its independent contractors, known as "Dashers," to improve their experience and ensure that gig work is a fair and sustainable way of earning a living. For example, DoorDash has implemented a "Dasher Deactivations Appeal Process" that allows Dashers to challenge deactivations from the platform and have their cases reviewed by a third party. DoorDash has also introduced a "Dasher Pay Protection" policy, which provides additional compensation to Dashers with problematic orders.

Some will argue that gig work is insecure and lacks the benefits and protections of traditional employment. In response, DoorDash has implemented a "Dasher Bill of Rights" that outlines the rights and responsibilities of Dashers on the platform, and has set up a "Dasher Support" team to provide assistance and resources to Dashers. Overall, DoorDash is committed to working with its Dashers to make the gig work experience better and address any challenges that may arise.

Tales From the Delivery Dark Side

As a DoorDash driver, I've had my fair share of interesting deliveries, but none quite like this one. It was a beautiful Saturday afternoon, and I was feeling pretty good about the shift ahead. That all changed when I received an order for delivery to a swanky mansion in Beverly Hills. I figured it was just another wealthy client, and eagerly made my way over to the address. When I arrived, I was buzzed in and made my way through the mansion's grand entrance. Just as I was about to knock, the door swung open, revealing a major motion picture star in all their glamorous glory. "Where's my food?" they barked, looking me up and down with disdain. I tried to speak but nothing came out. They literally snatched the food out of my hands and slammed the door in my face, leaving me standing on the doorstep feeling humiliated and deflated. On top of that, the tip was only $3.00—no unicorns today.

Chapter 2:
Understanding the DoorDash Platform

Understanding the DoorDash platform is an important aspect of becoming a successful DoorDash driver. As we noted earlier, DoorDash is a delivery app that connects drivers with customers who need items delivered to their location. As a DoorDash driver, you will use the app to accept and complete orders, communicate with customers, and track your earnings. You will spend 100% of your time inside of the DoorDash app when driving and delivering for the service.

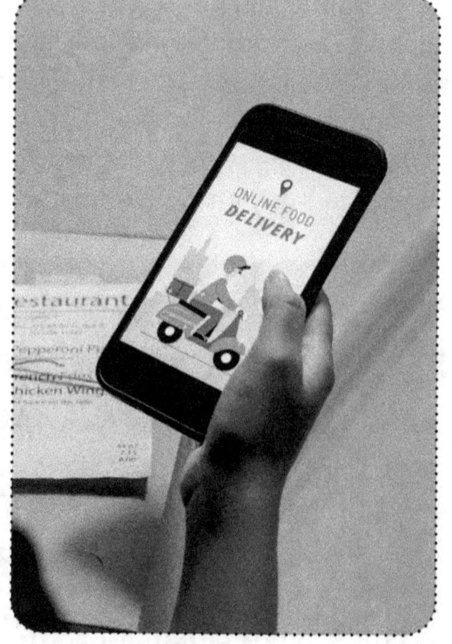

To understand the DoorDash platform, it is important to familiarize yourself with the various features and tools that the app offers. This includes the dashboard, which displays your current and past orders, as well as your earnings and ratings. You should also understand how to accept and complete orders, and how to communicate with customers through the app's messaging feature. It is also important to understand DoorDash's payment system, which determines how much you earn for each delivery and how you are paid. Later in this book, we will cover a great deal of these topics in more detail.

Understanding the DoorDash platform will not only help you navigate the app more efficiently, but it will also help you make the most of your time as a

DoorDash driver. In this chapter, we will provide a detailed overview of the DoorDash platform and its various features, as well as tips for using the app effectively.

The DoorDash Dashboard

The DoorDash dashboard is an important feature of the app that allows you to track your orders, earnings, and ratings as a Dasher. When you open the DoorDash app, the dashboard is typically the first screen you will see. It displays a range of information and tools that are essential for managing your deliveries and earning money as a DoorDash driver. The DoorDash driver app can be downloaded for Android or Apple iPhone devices. Don't get this app confused with the main DoorDash app, which is used by the customer to place the order.

The DoorDash dashboard includes several key sections:

Current orders: This section displays any orders that you have currently accepted and are in the process of delivering. It shows the pickup location, delivery location, and estimated time of arrival for each order.

Past orders: This section displays a history of your completed orders, including the date, time, and location of each delivery. You can use this section to track your earnings and review your ratings from customers.

Earnings: This section displays your total earnings as a Dasher, as well as any bonuses or incentives that you have earned. It also includes information on how much you have earned in the current pay period and how much you have earned in total.

Ratings: This section displays your overall rating as a Dasher, as well as the number of ratings you have received. A high rating is important for maintaining a good reputation on the platform and getting more orders.

The DoorDash Acceptance Rate

The **DoorDash acceptance rate** refers to the percentage of orders that a Dasher accepts out of the total number of orders they receive. DoorDash considers a high acceptance rate to be an important factor in determining the reliability and performance of its Dashers. As a Dasher, it is important to maintain a high acceptance rate in order to maintain a good reputation on the platform and increase your chances of getting more orders.

There are a few key factors that can impact your DoorDash acceptance rate:

- **Timely response:** It is important to be timely and responsive when receiving an order notification. The faster you respond, the more likely you are to get the order.

- **Order location:** Consider the distance and duration of the delivery when deciding whether to accept an order. If the pickup or delivery location is too far or would take too long to complete, it may not be worth accepting the order. Think about the current situation at the restaurant as well; certain restaurants may be understaffed, or, have the lobby closed which means you have to wait in a busy drive-thru.

- **Order details:** Review the details of the order carefully before accepting it. They don't give you all the information you may need to make a decision, so, you have to really think these orders over. (see the floating widget hack above to help with this).

- **Personal availability:** Consider your personal availability and schedule when deciding whether to accept an order. If you are not able to complete the delivery within the estimated time of arrival, it may be best to decline the order.

By keeping these factors in mind, you can maintain a high DoorDash acceptance rate and increase your chances of getting more orders on the platform.

Also, DoorDash may offer you "Top Dasher" status if you have a high acceptance rate. The "Top Dasher" program from DoorDash is a rewards program that recognizes and rewards top-performing Dashers on the platform.

To be eligible for the program, Dashers must maintain a high acceptance rate, a high rating from customers, and complete a certain number of deliveries per month. Top Dashers are eligible for a range of benefits and perks, including higher payment rates for deliveries, being able to deliver without pre-scheduling, exclusive promotions and bonuses, and special recognition on the DoorDash platform.

The "Top Dasher" program was designed to recognize and reward the most reliable and high-performing Dashers on the platform. By maintaining a high acceptance rate, a high rating from customers, and completing a high number of deliveries, Dashers can increase their chances of becoming a Top Dasher and be able to enjoy the benefits and perks that come with it.

FAST FACTS ABOUT DOORDASH

DoorDash is currently available in over 4,000 cities in the United States and Canada.

DoorDash has partnerships with over 350,000 merchants and restaurants, allowing customers to order from a wide range of local and national brands.

DoorDash has been downloaded over 50 million times on the Google Play Store.

Tony Xu, Stanley Tang, Andy Fang, and Evan Moore, came up with the idea for DoorDash while working on a business school project.

Sample Incoming Order Screen

The decline button is how you decline an incoming order.

The map shows you where you are going.

You must deliver by this time, from this restaurant.

How many items you are delivering and how far it is.

The timer counts down as you consider taking the order.

How much you may be making (could be a higher amount which is not shown).

Hitting the accept button will start you on this order.

DoorDash uses a complex algorithm to determine the pay for each delivery. The algorithm takes into account a number of factors, including the distance of the delivery, the complexity of the order, the demand for delivery in the area, and the availability of Dashers (DoorDash drivers). DoorDash also uses the algorithm to determine which orders are offered to which Dashers, taking into account the Dasher's location, past performance, and ratings from customers. The algorithm is constantly being updated and refined to ensure that Dashers are fairly compensated and customers receive timely, high-quality service.

Chapter 3:
Applying to Become a DoorDash Driver

Applying to become a DoorDash driver is a straightforward process that involves completing an online application and meeting a few basic requirements. DoorDash is available in a number of cities across the United States, and the requirements for becoming a Dasher may vary depending on your location.

In general, the requirements for becoming a DoorDash driver include:

- **Age:** You must be at least 18 years old to apply to become a DoorDash driver.

- **Vehicle:** You must have access to a reliable vehicle to use for deliveries. DoorDash accepts a range of vehicle types, including cars, motorcycles, and bicycles.

- **Smartphone:** You must have a smartphone to use the DoorDash app and communicate with customers. There are both iPhone and Android apps available.

- **Background check:** DoorDash will conduct a background check as part of the application process. You must pass the background check in order to become a Dasher.

One interesting fact about DoorDash delivery drivers is that they are independent contractors, not employees. This means that DoorDash does not have the same level of control over their work as it would with traditional employees, and is not responsible for providing them with benefits such as health insurance or paid time off.

As a DoorDash driver, it is important to have the appropriate car insurance coverage to protect yourself and your vehicle while making deliveries. DoorDash requires that all Dashers have at least third-party liability coverage, which covers damages or injuries that you may cause to other people or their property while driving.

In addition to third-party liability coverage, it is also recommended that you have comprehensive and collision coverage to protect your own vehicle in the event of an accident or other damage. This type of coverage can help cover the cost of repairs or replacement if your vehicle is damaged while making deliveries.

It is important to check with your insurance provider to make sure that you have the appropriate coverage while driving for DoorDash. Some insurance policies may exclude coverage for commercial use, or may require you to purchase an endorsement to cover your activities as a Dasher.

To apply to become a DoorDash driver, follow these steps:

1. Go to the DoorDash website and click on the "Become a Dasher" link.

2. Enter your zip code and select your city to see if DoorDash is available in your area.

3. Click on the "Apply Now" button and follow the prompts to complete the online application.

4. Provide the required documentation, including proof of your age, vehicle insurance, and any other documents that may be required.

5. Wait for your application to be reviewed and approved. If your application is approved, you will receive an email with instructions on how to get started as a Dasher.

By following these steps, you can apply to become a DoorDash driver and start earning money by making deliveries in your area.

Chapter 4:
Completing the Onboarding Process

After your application to become a DoorDash driver has been approved, you will need to complete the onboarding process in order to start making deliveries. The onboarding process typically includes a combination of online training and possibly in-person orientation, depending on your market.

The online training component of the onboarding process typically includes video tutorials and quizzes that cover the basics of the DoorDash platform and how to make deliveries. This training will provide you with the information you need to get started as a Dasher and ensure that you are familiar with the app and the delivery process.

In addition to the online training, you may also be required to attend an in-person orientation session in your area. These sessions are typically led by a DoorDash representative and provide an opportunity to meet other Dashers, ask questions, and learn more about the company and the platform.

This is becoming more of a rarity due to the huge influx of new drivers. After you have completed the online training and any required in-person orientation sessions, you will be ready to start making deliveries as a DoorDash driver.

A good bit of advice is to watch a few YouTube videos about driving for DoorDash. There are a multitude of videos that will take you on drive-alongs with Dashers who have been driving for the platform for an extended amount of time. There are also a variety of Facebook groups for DoorDash drivers with tips and tricks, complaints, and recommendations about the service. These are all invaluable resources to look into before getting behind the wheel for your first delivery.

FAST FACTS ABOUT DOORDASH

DoorDash was founded in 2013 by four Stanford University students: Tony Xu, Stanley Tang, Andy Fang, and Evan Moore.

The company was initially called 'Palo Alto Delivery,' but was later renamed DoorDash.

DoorDash launched its first pilot program in Palo Alto, California in 2013, and quickly expanded to other cities in the San Francisco Bay Area.

DoorDash has received significant investment from venture capital firms and other investors, and is currently valued at over $16 billion.

DoorDash has faced criticism and legal challenges related to its business model and treatment of its drivers, including a class action lawsuit alleging that the company pays its drivers "substandard wages." Despite these challenges, the company has continued to grow and expand its operations in the United States and internationally.

Chapter 5:
Accepting and Completing Orders

As a DoorDash driver, you have the ability to accept or decline incoming orders through the app. When you receive an order notification, you will have a very limited amount of time to decide whether you want to accept it or not. It is important to be timely and responsive when making this decision, as orders are typically assigned to the first Dasher who accepts them.

DoorDash may send you a "stacked" order, which means that you will be picking up multiple orders for either multiple or single customers. For example, you may see an order come in that will ask you to pick up an order for Matt J. at Burger King, then travel to McDonalds to pick up an order for Mary M. These 2 orders are from different restaurants going to different customers at different locations. These stacked orders will give you slightly more time to accept or decline the order, but they require quite a bit more thought and foresight to pull them off correctly.

To accept an incoming DoorDash order:

When an order pops up on screen, you will have a few seconds to review the details of the order, including the pickup location, delivery location (without the physical address) with mileage, and estimated time of arrival.

If you are interested in accepting this order, tap the "Accept" button. Remember, there is a time-out on these orders, so, you have to think quickly.

Normally, you will not be able to see what items in the order that you are picking up–however, it will show you the number of items you are picking up. For example, if it says "3 items," that could mean 1 Fry, 1 Double Cheeseburger and 1 Coca Cola.

There is a pretty big cheat here if you have an Android phone. If you have turned on "Show Floating Widget" in the app settings, you can pop out to your Android home screen, click on the floating DoorDash widget and hit the "Show Information" slider button.

This will show you the entire order, including the actual street address & apartment number if applicable. This is a must-use trick if you have the proper phone to take advantage of it.

If you are still interested in accepting the order, tap the "Confirm" button.

To decline an incoming DoorDash order:

Carefully review the details of the order and decide if you would rather not accept it.

If you do not want to accept the order, tap the "Decline" button.

You will be asked to confirm your decision to decline the order and give a reason which DoorDash supposedly keeps track of in a database. Tap "Confirm" to finalize your decision.

It is important to note that declining orders too frequently may negatively impact your rating on the platform and make it more difficult to get orders in the future. This is known as your "**acceptance rate**," which we talked about in an earlier chapter.

To take, or not to take; that is the question.

As a DoorDash driver, you have the flexibility to choose which orders you accept and which orders you decline. While it may be tempting to accept as many orders as possible in order to maximize your earnings, it is important to consider a few factors when deciding whether to accept an order.

Here are a few tips for deciding which DoorDash orders to take or which orders to decline:

Consider the distance and duration of the delivery. Make sure that the pickup and delivery locations are within a reasonable distance and that you will be able to complete the delivery within the estimated time of arrival. If the delivery is too far or would take too long to complete, it may not be worth accepting the order.

Watch where the order will take you. if you end up in the middle of nowhere to make the delivery, you still will have to drive all the way back to your zone to take new orders. Your car will also be empty at this time which is known as "dead-heading." A better strategy is to try to take orders at one end of your zone with a lot of restaurants and choose deliveries that allow you to end up in another part of your zone with more restaurants in it.

Review the order details. Before accepting an order, review the details carefully to make sure you are comfortable with the items being delivered and any special instructions. If you are not comfortable with the items or the delivery instructions, you may want to decline the order. Also remember wait times at restaurants–if you're stuck in line waiting, you cannot accept any other orders at that time. Stay away from restaurants that have known wait times or are understaffed.

Consider your personal availability. Make sure that you are available and able to complete the delivery within the estimated time of arrival. If you're not able to complete the delivery within the estimated time, it may be best to decline the order.

By considering these factors, you can help ensure that you are able to complete successful deliveries and maintain a high acceptance rate on the DoorDash platform. This will allow you to secure better and higher-paying orders in the future.

Diamonds are a Dasher's Best Friend

The 'Top Dasher' program and the 'Diamond Dasher' program are both rewards programs from DoorDash that recognize and reward top-performing Dashers on the platform. The main difference between the two programs is the eligibility criteria and the level of benefits and perks that are offered.

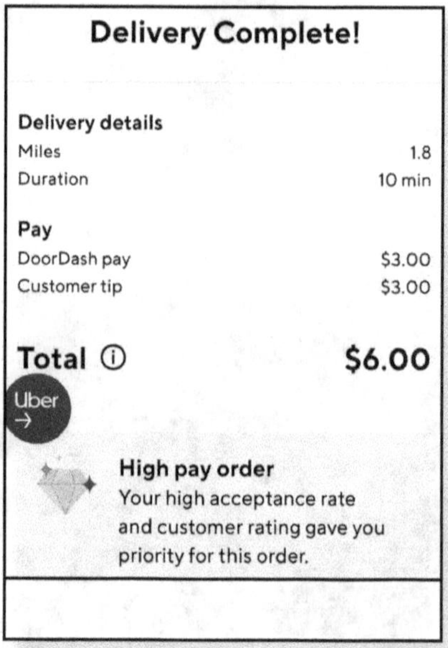

To be eligible for the Top Dasher program, Dashers must maintain a high acceptance rate, a high rating from customers, and complete a certain number of deliveries per month. Top Dashers are eligible for a range of benefits and perks, including higher payment rates for deliveries, exclusive promotions and bonuses, and special recognition on the DoorDash platform.

The Diamond Dasher program is a more exclusive rewards program that is reserved for the highest-performing Dashers on the platform. To be eligible for the Diamond Dasher program, Dashers must meet even more stringent criteria, including a higher number of deliveries per month and a higher rating from customers. Diamond Dashers are eligible for even more benefits and perks than Top Dashers, including higher payment rates and more exclusive promotions and bonuses.

Overall, both the Top Dasher and Diamond Dasher programs are designed to recognize and reward the most reliable and high-performing Dashers on the DoorDash platform. Depending on your market, these special programs may or may not be achievable–don't stress too much about them when you are starting out.

Why am I not getting any orders?

If you are not receiving any orders on the DoorDash driver's app, there are a few potential reasons why this may be happening. Here are a few possible explanations:

- **You may be in an area with low demand.** If you are in an area with low demand for deliveries, you may not receive as many orders as you would in a busier location. Consider moving to a different area or checking back at a later time when demand may be higher.

- **Your acceptance rate may be too low.** If you have a low acceptance rate, you may not receive as many orders as you would if your acceptance rate was higher. Consider accepting a higher percentage of orders that are offered to you to improve your acceptance rate.

- **Your customer rating may be too low.** If you have a low rating from customers, you may not receive as many orders as you would if your rating was higher. Consider improving your service and following any special instructions or requests provided by customers to improve your rating.

- **There may be technical issues.** If you are experiencing technical issues with the app, you may not be receiving orders as expected. Try contacting DoorDash support for assistance. Occasionally, the DoorDash service will be down completely. You will normally see an on-screen warning alerting you to the potential outage.

- **You may be having network or cellular issues.** Sometimes, you may be a in poorly covered cellular area. You can

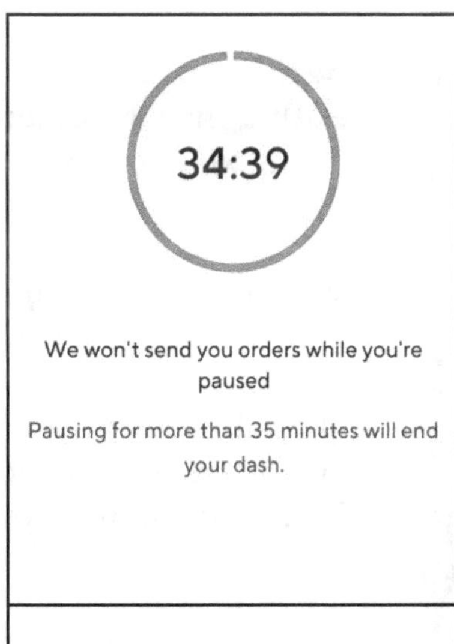

test this by browsing some random webpages on your phone–if they don't load, you may be having connectivity problems. Try restarting your phone or moving to a different location to improve your connectivity.

- **Your DoorDash app may be 'stuck' or paused.** If you decline a few orders in a row, DoorDash will most likely force your app to pause for awhile. You will be notified of this and you will have the option to unpause the app and continue your dash. If the app is stuck, you may not realize this and will have to usually either force restart the app, or, log out and then log back in to let DoorDash know you are online and ready for orders. This should only be used as a last resort, since if you log out and try to log back in, it may tell you there are no open Dashing spots–this is a gamble one way or the other.

> The top five menu items ordered on DoorDash in 2022 were French fries; burrito bowls and burritos; chicken nuggets and sandwiches; hash browns; and cheeseburgers.

FAST FACTS ABOUT THE GIG ECONOMY

The gig economy is a term used to describe the growing trend of people working on a freelance or temporary basis, often through online platforms or app-based companies.

The gig economy is believed to have originated in the early 2000s with the emergence of platforms like eBay, which allowed people to sell goods and services online.

The gig economy has grown significantly in recent years, with estimates suggesting that as much as 36% of the US workforce is now participating in gig work.

The gig economy is not limited to traditional "gig" jobs like driving or delivery, but also includes a range of other industries such as freelance writing, graphic design, and programming.

Chapter 6: Communicating with Customers

Effective communication with customers is an important aspect of being a successful DoorDash driver. The DoorDash app includes a messaging feature that allows you to communicate with customers throughout the delivery process. It is important to be timely and responsive when using this feature, as it can help ensure a smooth delivery and a positive customer experience.

Here are a few tips for communicating with your customers when driving for DoorDash:

- **Introduce yourself.** When you first receive an order notification, introduce yourself to the customer and confirm the details of the delivery. This may include the pickup location, delivery location, and estimated time of arrival. Not all Dashers adhere to this advice and many of them simply will only communicate if there is a problem or question with the order.

- **Keep the customer informed.** Keep the customer informed of your progress throughout the delivery process. For example, let them know when you have picked up the order, when you are on your way to the delivery location, and when you have arrived. Again, some Dashers will only do this step if there's an issue with the order. Use this communication feature to inform the customer of any problems with the order, including out-of-stock items.

- **Respond promptly.** Be timely and responsive when communicating with customers. If the customer has any questions or concerns, make

sure to address them as quickly as possible.

Be friendly and professional! Remember that you are representing DoorDash and your behavior reflects on the company. Be friendly and professional in all of your interactions with customers.

Reminders are important! Don't be afraid to send a reminder to turn on the front porch light (even though the app does this when a customer places an order), or to make sure all of the pets are safely secured inside the home.

Need help finding the place? Use this time to converse with the customer if you cannot find the drop-off location or need some hints on landmarks to help find the location. Also this is a good time to ask for gate codes for gated communities if the customer did not note it already.

As a DoorDash driver, it is important to be aware of and follow any special instructions or requests that your customers may have. These instructions and requests may be included in the form of "customer notes" within the DoorDash app. Customer notes are special instructions or requests that are included with an order by the customer. These notes may include requests for specific items to be included with the order, instructions for the pickup or delivery, or any other special requests.

It is important to review the customer notes carefully before accepting an order and to follow the instructions provided. Failing to follow customer notes may result in a negative rating or a cancellation of the order, which can impact your acceptance rate and earnings on the DoorDash platform. Before you send any communications to the customer, check these notes first–most often the answer is contained within them.

By following these basic tips, you can help ensure a smooth and successful delivery for your customers without any issues.

Chapter 7:
Earning Money and Getting Paid

How DoorDash Earnings Work

As a DoorDash driver, you have the opportunity to earn money by picking up and delivering orders to customers. DoorDash uses a dynamic pricing model, which means that the amount you earn for each delivery may vary depending on a variety of factors. These factors can include the distance of the delivery, the time of day, and the demand for deliveries in your area.

In addition to the base rate that you earn for each delivery, DoorDash also offers bonuses and incentives that can increase your earnings. These may include promotions for completing a certain number of deliveries in a given time period, or bonuses for delivering during high-demand periods. Holidays and special events in your area can bump up your base pay and can be found in the incentives area of the app. These incentives come and go, and the app will usually display an alert if there are incentives currently going on in your area.

DoorDash may also offer a *"Dasher Referral Program,"* which allows you to earn bonuses by referring other people to become Dashers on the platform. This may be dependent on your market.

On some orders, DoorDash may not show the full amount that you will be paid for the delivery. For example, you may see an order pop up that says you will make a guaranteed $6.50, however, when you finish the delivery you ended up making $13.75. This is known as a *"hidden tip,"* or some Dashers call them *"Unicorns."* These hidden tips are designed to thwart the 'cherry-pickers,' which are drivers who will only take the highest-paying orders, skipping over all of the smaller orders. By using this strategy, DoorDash can attract more drivers to pick up the smaller orders, because the driver assumes there may be a hidden tip on the order. Generally, these hidden tips usually are lurking on the $6.50 and higher orders, depending on the market. The good news is that you will never get paid less than the advertised rate shown on your screen.

Getting Paid By DoorDash

DoorDash uses a weekly payment schedule, which means that you will be paid on a weekly basis for the deliveries you have completed. The exact day of the week that you are paid will depend on the specific region you are in and the payment method you have chosen.

There are several payment options available to DoorDash drivers, including direct deposit, debit card, or check. DoorDash will automatically deposit your earnings into your chosen payment method each week, typically on the same day of the week. If you choose to be paid by check, you will need to allow extra time for the check to be mailed to you. And lastly, DoorDash offers a special debit card that you can have your earnings deposited to automatically and quickly.

It is important to note that DoorDash deducts a commission from each delivery, as well as any applicable taxes. The amount you are paid for each delivery will be the total order amount minus these deductions. DoorDash also provides a detailed breakdown of your earnings and deductions on the app and in your weekly earnings statement. Overall, DoorDash provides a convenient and reliable way for drivers to get paid for their deliveries.

DoorDash, Taxes and You.

As a DoorDash driver, you are considered an independent contractor rather than an employee, which means that you are responsible for paying your own taxes. DoorDash is required to report your earnings to the Internal

Revenue Service (IRS) and will send you a Form 1099-MISC at the end of the year that reports your total earnings for tax purposes.

It is important to keep track of your DoorDash earnings throughout the year and set aside a portion of your earnings to cover your tax liability. You

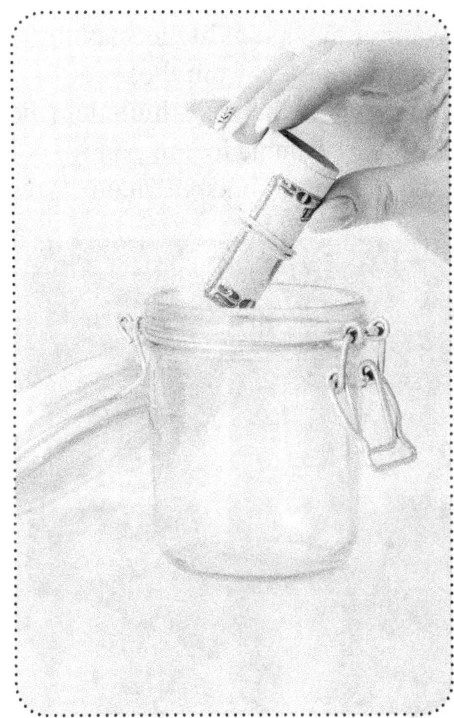

may also want to consider setting up a system to track your expenses, as you may be able to claim certain deductions on your taxes. For example, you may be able to deduct the costs of gas, maintenance, and other expenses related to your deliveries such as a pizza bag and drink holders. Mileage can also be deducted if you choose, and there are a few apps, such as **Gridwise**, that will track your mileage for you as you drive–and give you a total at the end of the year.

It is recommended that you consult with a tax professional or refer to IRS guidelines for more information on how taxes work for independent contractors. It is also a good idea to stay up to date on any changes to tax laws that may affect your tax liability as a DoorDash driver.

How to Earn the Most Money With DoorDash

As a DoorDash driver, there are several strategies you can use to maximize your earnings and make the most money delivering for DoorDash:

- **Accept more orders.** One of the simplest ways to maximize your earnings is to obviously accept as many orders as possible. By maintaining a high acceptance rate, you can increase your chances of receiving more orders and earning more money. This amounts to more driving and possible pickup and drop-off issues, but, it is a proven strategy for some of the busier markets.

- **Choose the right times to work.** Consider when demand for deliveries is highest in your area and try to work during these times. For example, busy lunch and dinner times may be more lucrative than slower periods of the day. Watch for incentives that pay more for peak delivery times.

- **Where to wait.** Find a personal 'hot zone' or 'home-base' and stay parked in that spot whenever possible. Waiting outside of higher-paying and busier restaurants will usually get you more orders from those restaurants. Busy zones are areas on the map where there is a high demand for deliveries and a limited number of Dashers available to complete the orders. These areas are indicated on the map by a "hotspot" icon and are typically located in busy commercial or residential areas. Accepting orders in busy zones can be a good way to maximize your earnings as a DoorDash driver. These orders are typically more lucrative and may have higher payment rates, as they are in high demand and there are fewer Dashers available to complete them. These zones update every 10 minutes and they are not set in stone.

- **Optimize your route.** Use the map and routing feature in the DoorDash app to plan the most efficient route between pickup and delivery locations.

- **Manage your expenses.** Keep track of your expenses, such as gas, maintenance, and other costs related to your deliveries. You may be able to claim some of these expenses as deductions on your taxes, which can help increase your net earnings.

By following these strategies and staying focused on maximizing your earnings–and driving smarter, you can make the most money delivering for DoorDash.

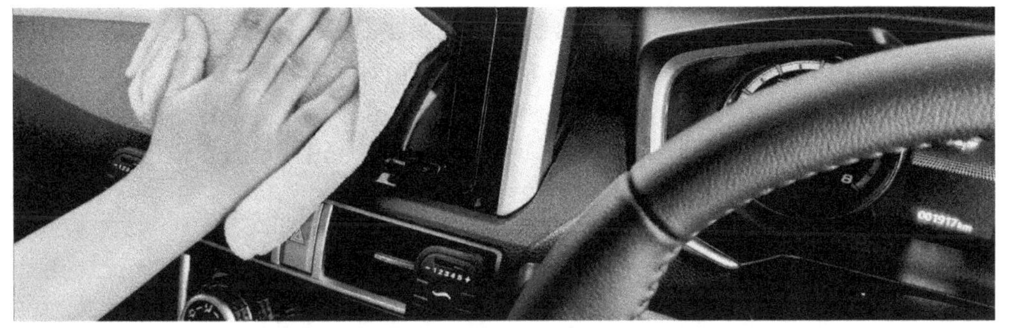

Chapter 8:
Staying Organized and Efficient

As a DoorDash driver, it's imperative to stay organized and efficient in order to maximize your earnings and provide a high-quality service to your customers. Here are a few tips for staying organized and efficient when driving for DoorDash:

- The DoorDash app provides a range of tools and features to help you stay organized and efficient, including a map and routing feature, a messaging feature for communicating with customers, and an order tracking feature. You can also use the app to track your earnings, acceptance rate and customer reviews. The app will also allow you to keep track of higher-paying incentives in your zone when available.

- Keep your vehicle organized and free of clutter to make it easier to find and retrieve items during deliveries. You may want to invest in a few storage solutions, such as a trunk organizer or seatback organizers, to help keep your vehicle organized. A 6-cup foldable drink holder and a pizza bag are a necessity to have in the car with you.

- Keep 2 coolers in your vehicle if you have the space. One cooler for hot items and one for cold items. In your cold cooler, consider a few plastic zipper bags of ice to keep ice cream and cold items ice cold. Look for some old clean towels to keep inside of your coolers to buffer things from moving around during travel.

- Plan your route in advance: Use the map and routing feature in the DoorDash app to plan the most efficient route between pickup and delivery locations. This can help you save time and increase the number of deliveries you can complete in a given period.

- Be prepared for unexpected delays. Try to anticipate and plan for potential delays, such as traffic or difficulty finding a parking spot at the pickup or delivery location. Remember which restaurants may have delays at pickup, or, have closed lobbies which requires you to sit in a long drive-thru line. By being prepared for unexpected delays, you can minimize the impact on your delivery schedule.

By following these tips and staying organized and efficient, you can help ensure a smooth and successful delivery process for your customers.

THE DOORDASH GLOSSARY

Dasher: A DoorDash driver who delivers food and other goods to customers at thier locations.

Order: A request for delivery made by a customer through the DoorDash app.

Pickup: The process of collecting an order from a restaurant or other merchant for delivery to the customer.

Delivery: The process of delivering an order.

Dash: A delivery made by a DoorDash driver.

Unicorn: A 'hidden' tip that is not shown until after you deliver the order

Getting 'Bobbied': If you get any food or drink for free while dashing, you post a selfie of you with it. It was named after a Dasher named Bobby who used to post these online.

Chapter 9:
Handling Difficult Deliveries and Customers

As a DoorDash driver, you may encounter problematic customers from time to time. These customers may be rude, uncooperative, or difficult to deal with, and can make the delivery process more challenging. Here are a few tips for dealing with problematic customers when driving for DoorDash:

- If you encounter a problem or issue with a delivery, try to communicate with your customer as soon as possible. This may involve calling or messaging them through the DoorDash app to resolve any issues or clarify any misunderstandings.

- Always take a photo of your drop-off and try to include the customer's house number if applicable, or other visual clues to help the customer and DoorDash figure out where the order was delivered in case of a mistake. DoorDash does not like mistakes, especially when you deliver the order to the wrong house.

- Make sure to review and follow any special instructions or requests provided by the customer. This may include requests for specific items to be included with the order, instructions for the pickup or delivery, or any other special requests.

- Even if a customer is being difficult, it is

important to remain calm and professional. Try not to take their behavior personally and do your best to maintain a respectful and courteous demeanor. Save any text messages or chat messages that they may send you.

• Try not to take matters too much into your own hands–if the restaurant made a mistake with the order, DoorDash and the restaurant are the ones at fault–all you can do is report whatever you can to make sure everything is documented. Make sure to let the customer know that they can report a missing or wrong item right inside of the DoorDash application.

• If you are unable to resolve a problem or issue with a delivery, you can contact DoorDash support for assistance. DoorDash has a team of customer service representatives available to help resolve any issues that may arise during a delivery.

• There is a built-in safety tool that allows Dashers to report any safety concerns or incidents that they may encounter while making deliveries. This may include accidents, injuries, suspicious activity, or any other safety concerns.

By following these tips and staying calm and professional, you can help ensure a smooth and successful delivery process even in the most difficult situations.

TALES FROM THE DELIVERY DARK SIDE

It was a hot and humid summer day, and I was feeling a bit grumpy after a long shift. That all changed when I received an order for delivery to a local zoo. I figured it would be a fun and unique experience, and eagerly made my way over to the zoo. When I arrived, I was greeted by a group of chimpanzees who seemed to be having a bit too much fun. As I was making my way through the zoo, they started tossing banana peels and other debris at me, causing me to duck and weave to avoid getting hit. Just when I thought things couldn't get any worse, I stumbled upon a group of gorillas who seemed to be having a territorial dispute. I tried to make a quick exit, but one of the gorillas reached out and grabbed the food bag out of my hands and ran off, leaving me empty-handed and covered in banana peels. It was definitely the worst delivery experience of my career.

Chapter 10:
Maintaining a Good Rating on the DoorDash Platform

The DoorDash rating system is a way for customers to rate the performance of Dashers and provide feedback on their experience. After each delivery, customers are asked to rate their Dasher on a scale of 1 to 5 stars inside of the app, with 5 stars being the highest rating. Customers can also leave a written review or comment about their experience, which will eventually make their way to the Dasher's dashboard.

As a Dasher, your rating is an important factor in your success on the DoorDash platform. A high rating can make you more attractive to customers and increase your chances of getting more orders. A low rating, on the other hand, can make it more difficult to get orders and may impact your overall earnings. Some Dashers have taken steps to improve ratings, such as printing out rating reminder stickers that are placed on each order, or, providing extras such as packets of condiments and straws with orders. Communicating with the customer about late deliveries can also help ratings, as we talked about earlier.

To maintain a high rating on DoorDash, it is important to provide excellent service to customers and go above and beyond to meet their needs. This may include being punctual, friendly, and helpful, as well as being willing to go the extra mile to ensure a smooth delivery. Dashers can really use their imaginations to come up with other fun and unique ways to improve customer ratings.

In addition to maintaining a good rating, it is also important to maintain a high acceptance rate on the DoorDash platform. A high acceptance rate means that you are accepting a high percentage of orders that are offered to you, which can increase your chances of receiving more orders and earning more money.

Keeping a good acceptance rate

Here are five tips for maintaining a high acceptance rate:

- Try to accept orders as soon as they are offered to you. This can help ensure that you are able to complete the maximum number of deliveries and maximize your earnings.

- If you have any questions or concerns about an order, make sure to communicate with the customer as soon as possible. This can help prevent misunderstandings and ensure a smooth and successful delivery.

- Make sure to review and follow any special instructions or requests provided by the customer.

- Make sure to arrive at the pickup and delivery locations on time and follow the correct delivery route. This can help maintain a high rating from customers and increase your chances of receiving more orders.

- Make sure to keep your vehicle clean and well-maintained, as this can help ensure that you are able to complete deliveries without any issues.

Remember, DoorDash sets a minimum acceptance rate for its Dashers, and if a Dasher's acceptance rate falls below this minimum, DoorDash may deactivate their account. The specific minimum acceptance rate may vary depending on the market and other factors, but generally speaking, DoorDash expects its Dashers to maintain a high acceptance rate in order to ensure that orders are fulfilled efficiently and in a timely manner.

If you are having trouble maintaining a high acceptance rate, it is a good idea to try to identify the reasons why you may be rejecting orders and see if there are any steps you can take to improve your acceptance rate.

By following these tips and providing high-quality service to your customers, you can maintain a good rating on the DoorDash app and increase your chances of success as a Dasher.

TALES FROM THE DELIVERY DARK SIDE

As a DoorDash driver, I had seen my fair share of challenging deliveries, but nothing could have prepared me for my worst delivery experience. It was a hot summer day, and I was already running behind schedule when I received an order for a large group of people at a remote location outside of town. The address was difficult to find, and I ended up getting lost on the winding country roads.

By the time I finally arrived at the destination, the food was cold and the customer was livid. They demanded a full refund and refused to pay for the order, even though it was clearly stated in the app that there would be no refunds for late deliveries. I tried to explain the situation and offer to redeliver the order, but the customer was having none of it.

To make matters worse, as I was leaving, my car broke down on the side of the road. I had to call a tow truck and spend the rest of the night waiting for it to arrive, all while being berated by the angry customer on the phone. It was easily the worst delivery experience of my career!

Chapter 11:
Tips and Tricks for DoorDash Success

As a DoorDash driver, there are several known tips and tricks you can use to increase your chances of success on the platform. Here are a few strategies you can use to improve your performance as a Dasher:

- **Accept as many orders as possible.** One of the simplest ways to maximize your earnings is to accept as many orders as possible. By maintaining a high acceptance rate, you can increase your chances of receiving more orders and earning more money.

- **Pick and choose which orders are best for you and your market.** Consider taking an order if you can make at least $1.00-$2.00 per mile, depending on the market. There's really no point to take a $4.00 order that is making you drive 18 miles to deliver it and then return back to your home-base.

- **Location, Location, Location.** Try to take orders that send you to another area with more restaurants. If you take an order that sends you to the middle of nowhere, you will still have to drive all the way back to your starting point to get more orders and your car will be empty.

- **Choose the right times to work.** Consider when demand for deliveries is highest in your area and try to work during these times. For example, busy lunch and dinner times may be more lucrative than slower periods of the day.

- **Optimize your route.** Use the map and routing feature in the DoorDash app to plan the most efficient route between pickup and delivery locations. This can help you save time and increase the number of deliveries you can complete in a given period.

- **Manage your expenses.** Keep track of your expenses, such as gas, maintenance, and other costs related to your deliveries. You may be able to claim some of these expenses as deductions on your taxes, which can help increase your net earnings.

- **Stay organized and efficient.** Use the tools and features in the DoorDash app to stay organized and efficient, and consider investing in a few storage solutions to keep your vehicle organized.

- **Keep your hands clean and keep your distance.** Keep a large container of hand sanitizer in the vehicle, up front and ready. You need to remember to keep your hands clean after leaving every restaurant and touching every food bag. This is critical to keep yourself healthy during and after Dashes. You will be around a lot of people and a lot of germs, especially during the winter months when flu season is raging.

- **Cleanup in aisle back seat.** Keep paper towels and wet-wipes in the car for cleaning up any spills. Consider large plastic bins for keeping orders organized, separated and away from your car's interior if you don't use coolers.

- **Run out the clock.** Make a list of the DoorDash order cutoff times which can be found in the customer's DoorDash app for each restaurant.

- **Branding is everything.** Consider wearing a DoorDash t-shirt or hoodie– most often when the restaurant workers see the DoorDash logo, they instantly know why you are there and will most often prioritize you over regular customers. These items can be found on the official DoorDash store, or on sites such as eBay, Redbubble, Amazon and Etsy. This seems to be a hot-button topic among Dashers–you either love the idea, or hate it, but, it does work regardless.

- **Float on.** Remember to use the floating widget if applicable on your device. This widget will tell you the actual delivery address as well as what food items are actually contained in the order.

- **Wrangling those bags.** Keep a stapler and extra staples in your vehicle to staple bags closed for easier handling.

- **Stay hydrated and full.** Don't forget your own snacks and drinks to keep you going throughout your shift. Don't give your hard-earned profits back to the very restaurants you are picking up from.

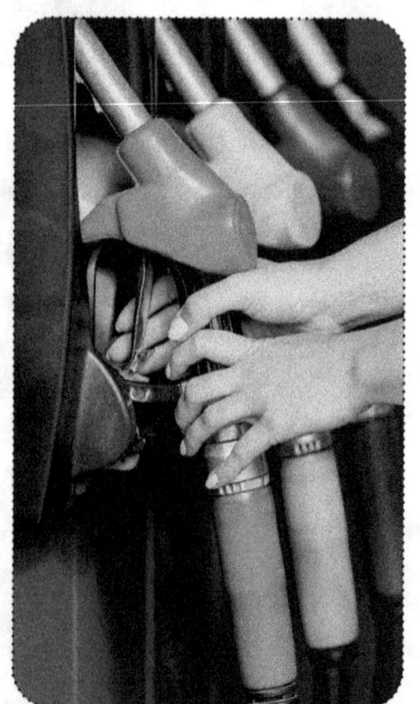

- **Nature calls–sometimes very often.** Have a good idea on where public restrooms are located when driving.

- **Keep up on your supplies.** Ask your favorite restaurants for extra supplies such as straws, silverware, sauces, salt and pepper, recyclable drink carriers and bags. They most often will give you as much as you need.

- **Positivity goes a long way.** Get friendly with the workers behind the counters–they will be more apt to get your orders out faster if you are nice to them. A simple "please" and "thank you" goes a long way here.

- **Diagrams can save lives.** Make a paper diagram of tricky apartment complexes and buildings that are difficult to navigate through. Keep these diagrams handy to help you navigate these mazes.

- **See the light.** Have a small battery-powered flashlight nearby for nighttime deliveries which won't burn out your phone's battery.

- **Backups are critical.** Have a backup charger and cable in your car for your phone.

- **Dead batteries are a bummer.** Consider a portable jump-start device in case you run your battery down waiting on orders.

- **What's the rush?** Don't drive like a race car driver; You will only introduce more wear and tear, higher gas usage and possibly get into an accident by driving as fast as you can. There is a clock running against you, however, DoorDash builds in as much time as you need to get the order delivered. This is a critical mistake that most new Dashers make

and is easily fixable. Check to make sure your license, insurance information and registration is up to date and located in the glove box in case you ignore this point. Also keep a few writing utensils and some paper with you in case of an accident.

- **A personal touch.** Personal stickers with a 'thank you' and a rating reminder go a long way and are cheap to make at home.

- **It's OK to wear the red.** Wear DoorDash branded items such as DoorDash t-shirts and hats to stand out from the public when you arrive at a restaurant. The restaurant staff will know instantly that you're not a customer waiting to order and will often prioritize you over the public.

- **Downtime is productive time.** While waiting for your order, look up the delivery address on Google maps which will usually give you a quick visual idea of the house you are looking for.

- **I'll be here all week.** Use the built-in scheduling feature in the DoorDash app to schedule yourself for the upcoming week before everyone else takes those spots.

- **Ask for help.** If there is a problem with a pickup after you accept an order, such as a store that is closed or a problem at the restaurant completing the order, don't un-assign yourself. Instead, contact DoorDash support and explain what is going on–often they can un-assign you (which doesn't hurt your acceptance rate) and sometimes give you half-pay for your efforts.

- **Baby, it's cold out outside.** Whenever you are parked and waiting on orders, consider turning off your car's engine. Try to get used to not using air conditioning whenever possible, which will save you big on gas. Buying a small clip-on fan plugged into a small rechargeable power station can help with summer heat. In the winter months, dress warmer than usual and try to use the heat in small doses, keeping the engine off when waiting for long stretches. This is a discipline thing and you can adapt after awhile.

- **There's an upside to everything.** Use the Upside app when getting gas, which gives you cash back into your bank account.

- **Fetch, spot, fetch.** Use the Fetch app which gives you points after scanning all of your receipts when driving. Any receipt will do including grocery and gas receipts. These points are redeemable for gift cards from various retailers, including Amazon.

- **Save yourself (and others, too!)** Always keep an emergency kit in your vehicle, including a simple first aid kit, aspirin, extra water bottles, battery charger cables, a small basic toolkit, a roll of duct tape for emergency repairs, a roll of toilet paper & paper towels, an extra set of clothing, extra warm clothing in the winter months (gloves, hats, 'Hot Hands' hand warmers), extra battery packs & cables for emergency phone charging. Learn how to change a flat tire on your vehicle, making sure you have easy

> **"Don't drive like a race car driver; You will only introduce more wear and tear, higher gas usage and possibly get into an accident by driving as fast as you can."**

access to the jack and spare tire. Have some work gloves and rags handy. Consider a flashing emergency light in case you get stuck. A small folding shovel for snowy conditions is wise to have on hand.

- **Can you hear me now?** Consider letting others know before you go out on a shift, in case you get stuck down a desolate dirt road–you may not have cellular service in some rural areas.

- **Take care of your baby.** You won't get too far if your vehicle gives up on you. This means that you need to pay extra special attention to it, such as regular tire rotations & tread checks, oil changes, gas treatments, windshield wipers, and air and cabin filter changes. Drive a little more gingerly, without falling into jack-rabbit starts, hard and fast turns and hard braking habits. You will get to your destination on time without resorting to these bad tactics. You may have to give up and extra delivery or 2 per hour when driving a little bit easier, but, your vehicle will thank you for it.

- **Take the good with the bad.** When driving for DoorDash, remember that you can't have a killer drive every time. You will undoubtedly have a day or 2 during your week that are just awful. No orders, no money, no nothing. This is normal and you just need to take these bad days with a grain of salt. Remember, DoorDash is flooding the markets with more and more drivers looking to make easy money, just like yourself. Between this and the state of the economy, and even what time of the month it happens to be is going to dictate how well you do when driving. It will be easy to blame yourself if you have a string of awesome days, and then it all goes to Hell on one shift. Don't fall into this trap–there are just a lot of variables in this gig that you have zero control over. Don't stress on these bad days and remember that you can just get in the car and do it all over again tomorrow, while learning from this bad shift.

MARKET SHARE OF MAJOR FOOD DELIVERY SERVICES IN THE UNITED STATES (SINCE 2022)

DoorDash: 50%
Grubhub: 30%
Uber Eats: 10%
Postmates: 5%
Other: 5%

TALES FROM THE DELIVERY DARK SIDE

As a DoorDash driver, I've had my fair share of challenging deliveries, but none quite like this one. It was a busy Friday night, and I was rushing to complete as many orders as possible. One order in particular stood out, with a long list of special requests and instructions. I carefully followed all of the instructions, making sure to get everything just right. When I arrived at the customer's house, I was greeted by a group of rowdy college students, in various states of undress, who seemed a bit worse for wear. I handed over the order, and watched as they tore into the food with reckless abandon. Just as I was about to leave, one of the students stumbled over and handed me a crumpled bill. "Keep the change," he slurred, before stumbling back to join his friends. As I made my way back to my car, I couldn't help but laugh at the absurdity of the whole situation. It was definitely the worst delivery of my career as a Dasher, but one that I'll always remember with a smile.

Chapter 12:
The Future of Delivery and the Gig Economy

The *gig economy*, which refers to the trend of companies hiring independent contractors or freelancers for short-term or flexible work such as DoorDash, has seen significant growth in recent years, particularly in the food delivery industry. This trend is likely to continue in the future as more and more people turn to food delivery apps for convenient and safe ways to have meals delivered to their homes. If there happens to be any more pandemic-level events in the future, this will only reinforce the use of this trend of home-delivery apps.

A futuristic McDonalds drive-through in Fort Worth, Texas in 2022

The use of autonomous robots, drones, self-driving vehicles, and AI automation in the food delivery space has the potential to significantly change the landscape of the entire industry in the future.

As of late 2022, there are already a few restaurant concepts that are either eliminating the order counter and internal seating in favor of more automation. McDonalds is field testing one of these stores called a "Take Away" store in Fort Worth, Texas as of this writing. In this futuristic store, they have ordering kiosks, an 'order-ahead lane' that serves customers through a conveyor belt system, no internal seating and pickup bays inside the store for DoorDashers and customer pickups. All ordering is done through the customer's phone or on the internal kiosks.

One potential benefit of using these technologies is increased efficiency and speed of delivery. For example, self-driving delivery vehicles or drones could potentially deliver orders more quickly than human drivers, especially in areas with heavy traffic or challenging road conditions. These vehicles also don't get tired, won't say no to low-paying orders or need bathroom breaks.

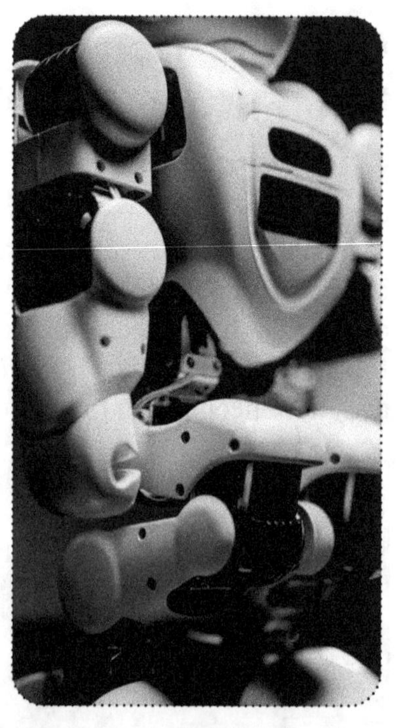

Another potential benefit is the reduction of labor costs. Automation and the use of robots or drones could potentially reduce the need for human delivery drivers, which could result in cost savings for companies.

However, the adoption of these technologies is likely to be gradual and will depend on a variety of factors, such as the cost of the technology, regulatory hurdles, and consumer acceptance. There is also the possibility that the use of these technologies could result in job loss for human delivery drivers. It's still too early to predict exactly how these technologies will change the landscape of the food delivery industry in the future, but they have the potential to significantly disrupt the industry even further.

Overall, it is difficult to predict exactly what the future of food delivery and the gig economy will look like. However, it is likely that the industry will continue to evolve and change as technology advances and consumer demands shift. While these trends may ebb and flow, your own future in the gig economy should be a positive and worthwhile endeavor going forward, even with the influx of new drivers flooding the roads. If you stick to the basics and become a smart delivery driver, you can easily rise above the incoming crowd of drivers, who may only be in the market for a short time before giving up and moving on.

According to a study conducted in 2020, the average DoorDash delivery driver earns about $14 per hour. However, the pay for a DoorDash delivery driver can vary significantly based on a number of factors, including the distance of the delivery, the complexity of the order, and the demand for delivery in the area.

Don't keep all your eggs in one basket!

Even though this book is primarily about the DoorDash platform, there are many different delivery driving gig options available in addition to DoorDash.

A majority of delivery drivers will typically "multi-app," which means they will run a few of these apps simultaneously when doing a driving shift. Some other popular delivery gig companies include:

- **Grubhub** is a food delivery company that allows you to deliver food from local restaurants to customers.

- **Postmates** is a delivery company that allows you to deliver a variety of items, including groceries, food, and household essentials.

- **Uber Eats** is a food delivery service that allows you to deliver food from local restaurants to customers using your own car or a car provided by Uber.

- **Instacart** is a grocery delivery service that allows you to deliver groceries to customers from local stores.

- **Amazon Flex** is a delivery service that allows you to deliver packages for Amazon using your own car.

- **Walmart Spark** is a delivery service that allows you to deliver groceries and items from Walmart using your own car.

These are just a few examples of the many delivery gig options available. In addition to these companies, there may be other local delivery services in your area that you can consider as well. Our advice is to sign-up for as many as possible and try them all–different markets are going to see different results when using various apps.

Chapter 13: In Closing

As this book comes to an end, you have hopefully learned some good tips, tricks and strategies for becoming a DoorDash delivery driver. The best advice is to just go out and start driving–yes, you may screw up the first few orders, but, as you get your rhythm down and your confidence increases, you will find yourself accomplishing your goal of making some extra money as a gig worker.

As a DoorDash driver, it is important to be organized and efficient in order to make the most of your time and earn the most money possible. One way to do this is by planning your routes ahead of time and using a mapping app to find the most efficient routes. It is also helpful to familiarize yourself with the areas you will be delivering to, so you can find your way around and make deliveries more quickly.

In addition to being organized and efficient, it is also important to be safe on the road and take care of your vehicle–baby it, if you will. Always follow traffic laws and be mindful of other drivers, and make sure to take breaks when you need to in order to stay alert and focused. Keeping your car clean and organized can also help you deliver orders more efficiently and effectively.

While driving and delivering for DoorDash can be a flexible and convenient way to earn money, it is important to remember that it is also a job and should be treated as such. Make sure to follow all relevant laws and regulations, and always prioritize safety above all else.

Overall, driving and delivering for DoorDash can be a rewarding experience that allows you to set your own schedule and earn money on your own terms. With a little organization and a focus on safety, you can be a successful DoorDash driver and enjoy the freedom and flexibility that the gig economy has to offer.

I hope we gave you some good information and food for thought, without burying you in an avalanche of information. Remember, this was designed as a getting-started guide to driving for DoorDash. Feel free to use your online resources for deeper information on this topic, and by all means, just get out and try it once or twice. You will know within this time period if this is a good fit for you or not.

Here's to your future in the gig economy–congratulations on getting this far already. I have full confidence in the fact that you can go out and do this and remember, we all had to start with our first delivery. Enjoy the rush that you will get by performing a unique service and making some easy money while doing it. You will get to use your brain and analytical mind to choose the best runs for you and sort through a lot of factors before taking those orders.

Definitely have fun out there, make all the money and stay safe!

www.ingramcontent.com/pod-product-compliance
Lightning Source LLC
Chambersburg PA
CBHW060921130726

48001CB00006B/2340